ideals®
FRIENDSHIP

More Than 50 Years of Celebrating Life's Most Treasured Moments

Vol. 54, No. 4

*"Hold a true friend
with both your hands."*

—*African Proverb*

IDEALS—Vol. 54, No. 4 July MCMXCVII IDEALS (ISSN 0019-137X) is published six times a year: January, March, May,
July, September, and November by IDEALS PUBLICATIONS INCORPORATED,
535 Metroplex Drive, Suite 250, Nashville, TN 37211.
Periodical postage paid at Nashville, Tennessee, and additional mailing offices.
Copyright © MCMXCVII by IDEALS PUBLICATIONS INCORPORATED.
POSTMASTER: Send address changes to Ideals, PO Box 305300, Nashville, TN 37230. All rights reserved.
Title IDEALS registered U.S. Patent Office.

SINGLE ISSUE—U.S. $5.95 USD; Higher in Canada
ONE-YEAR SUBSCRIPTION—U.S. $19.95 USD; Canada $36.00 CDN (incl. GST and shipping); Foreign $25.95 USD
TWO-YEAR SUBSCRIPTION—U.S. $35.95 USD; Canada $66.50 CDN (incl. GST and shipping); Foreign $47.95 USD

The cover and entire contents of IDEALS are fully protected by copyright and must not be reproduced in any manner whatsoever.

Printed and bound in USA by Quebecor Printing. Printed on Weyerhaeuser Husky.

The paper used in this publication meets the minimum requirements of
American National Standard for Information Sciences—
Permanence of Paper for Printed Library Materials, ANSI Z39.48-1984.

Subscribers may call customer service at 1-800-558-4343 to make address changes.
Unsolicited manuscripts will not be returned without a self-addressed, stamped envelope.

ISBN 0-8249-1144-X GST 131903775

Cover Photo
GLADIOLA ON A SUMMER'S EVE
Vision Impact Photography

Inside Front Cover
YOUNG GIRLS AT THE PIANO
Pierre-Auguste Renoir, artist (1841–1919)
Musée du Louvre, Paris
Bridgeman Art Library, London
Superstock

Inside Back Cover
FISHING FROM THE BRIDGE
William Kay Blacklock, artist (1872–1922)
Christie's, London
Superstock

August
Is a Copper Kettle

John C. Bonser

August is a copper kettle
Filled to brim with molten sun,
Pouring golden batter slowly
Till its griddlecakes are done.

August is a desert nomad
Traveling through an arid land,
Searching for some small oasis
In an endless stretch of sand.

August is a dreamer's knapsack
Packed with lazy, leisure days,
Strapped to Summer's sturdy shoulders
With the chords time's piper plays.

August, stay a little longer,
Let your heat becalm us all;
There are duties waiting for us
In the workplace of the fall!

LATE SUMMER ON THE FARM
Near Woodstock, Vermont
Gene Ahrens Photography

Summer's Afterglow

Loise Pinkerton Fritz

Just around this time of year,
I feel autumn in the air.
Though it's just late summertime,
I see many obvious signs
Of summer waning far and wide,
Ushering in the autumntide.

Fields are being harvested;
Apples on the trees are red.
Fledgling birds have left their nests;
In view are fairs and August fests.
Flowers have made their last-stand show,
Thus reflecting autumn's glow.
Evenings bring a touch of chill;
The morns are dew capped, autumn-still.

Just about this time of year,
I know that autumntime is near.
Though summer days are still in view,
The autumn scenes are peeking through.
Won't be long till all will know
It's autumn—summer's afterglow.

SUMMER TRANQUILITY
Brookline, Massachusetts
Dick Dietrich Photography

Autumn's Dawn

Patricia Sarazen

The fog lies thick upon the hill.
　　Dawn waits—tranquil, silent, and still.
The rabbit stirs amongst gold leaves
　　Where sleeping flowers interweave.

The joys of summer linger here
　　With all the blooms we hold so dear—
Forget-me-nots in heaven's blue,
　　Dianthus blooms so pink in hue.

The flowery mead spreads gold afar
　　To where the patterned fern beds are,
Beneath the trees all red and gold
　　Where gray stone walls stand ages old.

The fog lies thick upon the hill.
　　Dawn waits—tranquil, silent, and still.
A blissful day unveils its face
　　In golden, leafy, patterned lace.

GOLDENROD IN THE PASTURE
Cambridge, Vermont
William Johnson
Johnson's Photography

Overleaf Photograph
ROARING BROOK FALLS
Adirondack Mountains, New York
Jeff Gnass Photography

GIFTS

Mary Boyd Wagner

Ripening fruit upon the trees
In the August sun;
Cornfields swaying in the fields
When the day is done.
In her fairest garments dressed,
Nature, sweet and fair,
Ladles from earth's treasure chest
Gifts for all to share.

CORNUCOPIA
Gay Bumgarner

WALDEN POND
Near Concord, Massachusetts

Henry David Thoreau went to Walden Pond in 1845 seeking peace, solitude, and inspiration. From his two years, two months, and two days at this small Massachusetts pond came the book *Walden*, his journal of a solitary life in tune with nature. Not long ago I too went to Walden Pond, seeking a peaceful, natural retreat, and hoping for a glimpse of Henry Thoreau.

Ironically, in many ways, Walden today is even more natural than when Thoreau lived there. Thoreau chose Walden for his solitary retreat because it was a quiet, wooded spot within walking distance of his Concord, Massachusetts, home and because the land was owned by his dear friend Ralph Waldo Emerson. Thoreau found the inspiration he sought at Walden; but in addition to the birds and animals, he also shared the woods with railroad workers laying tracks to connect Concord to Boston, with ice cutters carving great chunks from the frozen pond for shipment to India, and with woodsmen thinning the forest to build homes and fuel fires. Today, even though suburban development squeezes in all around, Walden pond and its more than three hundred acres of woods are a protected sanctuary. The forests are thick again; and although Walden is a public state park today—a place for swimming, hiking, canoeing, and picnicking—access is controlled and limited. On a cloudless, but very cold, early morning in November, I found myself all but alone at Thoreau's pond.

A replica of the rustic cabin Thoreau built stands just yards away from the public parking area. Inside are representatives of his crude furnishings: a bed, a desk, a chair, and a woodstove. The true site of the cabin lies a half-mile away down a well-worn path through bare-limbed trees. The outline of the cabin's foundation lies near a pile of stones—a cairn begun by admirers of Thoreau's work in the years after his death. For more than one hundred years, visitors have laid stones on the pile in memory of Thoreau; each stone represents a life touched in some way by the words written on this very spot. I placed my own stone on the pile and stood back to reflect on Thoreau's oft-quoted words:

I went to the woods because I wished to live deliberately, to front out the essential facts of life and see if I could learn what it had to teach and not, when I came to die, discover that I had not lived.

Later, standing on the edge of the pond's icy waters, I was struck by the beauty of the spot. To the left rose Emerson Cliff, named for Thoreau's friend and mentor. The pond itself was quiet and still: the summer swimmers and boaters long gone and the water losing its battle with the coming winter and the spreading ice. All around, the banks rose up from the water's edge, creating a kind of natural amphitheater. It was cold and quiet and beautiful. I felt in harmony with nature. I felt close to Henry David Thoreau.

The Leaf

Mary D. Adams

I saw it drop from up so high,
Dancing against the autumn sky;
Graceful as it floated down,
Sighing when it touched the ground.

All summer it waved mid the trees,
Creating a ballet with every breeze.
Its points collected drops of rain;
The sun shone through its tiny veins.

A noble life, though brief and sweet,
Will end as a cushion for my feet.
A messenger from tree so tall
Sent to tell me it is fall.

BIG LEAF MAPLE
Near Alpine, Oregon
Dennis Frates/Oregon Scenics

LEGENDARY AMERICANS

NANCY J. SKARMEAS

RALPH WALDO EMERSON AND HENRY DAVID THOREAU

Often during his life, Ralph Waldo Emerson wrote about his desire to find a retreat from the distractions of daily life. He imagined a quiet cabin in the woods where he could live simply and devote himself to the experience of nature. In his journal in March of 1835, Emerson described the book he would write there, a "natural history of the woods around [the] shifting camp for every month of the year. . . . No bird, no bug, no bud should be forgotten in his day and hour." Ten years later, a rustic cabin was raised on land Emerson owned next to a quiet pond not far from his Massachusetts home. Tiny and crude, the cabin was to be the scene of the very experiment in simple living

that Emerson had long dreamed about. Except the cabin was built not by Emerson, but by his dear friend Henry David Thoreau. While Emerson carried on with his life as author, lecturer, husband, and father, Thoreau moved into the cabin on Walden Pond to seek the "essential facts of life." Out of this experience, of course, came *Walden*, Thoreau's beautiful journal of life in harmony with nature, a book that owes a great debt to the unique friendship between two brilliant men.

Emerson and Thoreau met in Concord, Massachusetts, in the fall of 1837. Although in literary history they are treated as contemporaries, they met on less than equal footing. Emerson at thirty-four was the author of the recently published book *Nature* and leader of the transcendentalist movement in American thought. Thoreau, only twenty, just out of Harvard, was an aspiring poet yet to make his voice heard. The two men, however, were drawn to each other. Emerson represented the continuation of the education Thoreau had begun at Harvard. Emerson was a man who shared a passion for ideas, who loved to talk and philosophize and to immerse himself in the beauty of nature. In Emerson, Thoreau saw his own future as a writer; and he quickly became a devoted disciple, so much so that many in Concord joked about how the younger man adopted not only the philosophy of his mentor but his speech and mannerisms as well.

But those who sneered did not understand the depth of the friendship, nor its balance. Whereas Thoreau found a mentor in Emerson, Emerson found a refreshing inspiration in Thoreau. Referring to Thoreau in his journal during the early days of their acquaintance, Emerson celebrated the young man's clarity of vision and the simplicity with which he lived his life. In his writings, Emerson urged men to ignore traditional authority and to seek truth through intuition and firsthand experience. Many years later, he would write that the young Thoreau was the incarnation of this philosophy. In 1837, their friendship just beginning, Emerson predicted great things for his young friend.

For twenty-five years, Emerson and Thoreau were close. They indulged each other's passion for ideas; they encouraged and criticized each other's writings. They took long walks in the woods and shared each other's rapture in the realm of nature. Together, they were at the heart of the renaissance in American literature that became known as the "flowering of New England." But ideas were not all they shared. Thoreau—who never married—cared for the Emerson children and served as a handyman around the family estate. When Emerson went on an extended lecture tour through Europe, Thoreau moved into his home to watch over his friend's ailing wife; and when Thoreau sought a quiet place to think and write, Emerson gladly offered the land around Walden Pond. The two men complemented each other: Emerson's philosophy found life in Thoreau, and Thoreau's life found stability in Emerson.

As the years passed, the friendship was touched by bitterness, and both men's private journals contained harsh words. Emerson, who was warm and emotional, decried Thoreau's cool and detached nature. And, sounding much like a disappointed father, he criticized Thoreau—who did not achieve broad acclaim in his lifetime—for his lack of ambition. Thoreau, for his part, often sounded equally disappointed. He faulted his friend for being so concerned with worldly matters that he had lost touch with the simple truths of life. In 1851, Thoreau wrote sadly of Emerson, "Even when I meet thee unexpectedly, I part from thee with disappointment. Though I enjoy thee more than other men, yet I am more disappointed with thou than others." Both men were two independent thinkers who lived their lives with passion and intensity. They saw their friendship as a special communion of souls and reached for a relationship that soared above the mundane. When they connected, it was inspirational; when they slipped into pettiness and discord, it was a painful disappointment.

Biographies of both men prove, however, that even while they were venting their anger and pain in their journals, they did not allow their friendship to break beyond repair. By the late 1850s, when Thoreau became ill with tuberculosis, the rift that had never been openly acknowledged was fully healed. As Thoreau's health failed, Emerson was frequently by his side; as always, they were talking—about writing, about nature, about experience, about life. Emerson eased his friend's final days.

At the funeral, Emerson gave a moving eulogy, which included his lament that his friend had not had the opportunity to leave his mark upon the world. Time, of course, has proven otherwise. *Walden*, the book Thoreau wrote in the tiny cabin built on his dear friend's land, the book which so eloquently describes the philosophy of life that Thoreau and Emerson shared, has carried Thoreau's voice to independent-minded thinkers in every walk of life for one hundred and fifty years. The two friends stand side by side in history as men of brilliance and influence.

At the end of his life, his mind failing, Emerson is said to have asked his wife to recall for him the name of his dearest friend. "Henry Thoreau," she answered. "Yes," Emerson agreed, "it was Henry Thoreau."

OUR HERITAGE

FROM *SELF-RELIANCE*

Ralph Waldo Emerson

There is a time in every man's education when he arrives at the conviction that envy is ignorance; that imitation is suicide; that he must take himself for better, for worse, as his portion; that though the wide universe is full of good, no kernel of nourishing corn can come to him but through his toil bestowed on that plot of ground which is given to him to till. The power which resides in him is new in nature, and none but he knows what that is which he can do, nor does he know until he has tried. Not for nothing one face, one character, one fact, makes much impression on him, and another none. This sculpture in the memory is not without pre-established harmony. The eye was placed where one ray should fall, that it might testify of that particular ray. We but half express ourselves, and are ashamed of that divine idea which each of us represents. It may be safely trusted as proportionate and of good issues, so it be faithfully imparted, but God will not have his work made manifest by cowards. A man is relieved and gay when he has put his heart into his work and done his best; but what he has said or done otherwise shall give him no peace. . . .

A foolish consistency is the hobgoblin of little minds, adored by little statesmen and philosophers and divines. With consistency a great soul has simply nothing to do. He may as well concern himself with his shadow on the wall. Speak what you think now in hard words; and to-morrow speak what to-morrow thinks in hard words again, though it contradict everything you said to-day.— "Ah, so you shall be sure to be misunderstood."— Is it so bad, then, to be misunderstood? Pythagoras was misunderstood, and Socrates, and Jesus, and Luther, and Copernicus, and Galileo, and Newton, and every pure and wise spirit that ever took flesh. To be great is to be misunderstood.

ABOUT THE AUTHOR

Ralph Waldo Emerson was born on May 25, 1803, in Boston, Massachusetts. After graduating from Harvard College, Emerson studied briefly at the Harvard Divinity School; in 1829 he was ordained as a minister at the Second Church in Boston. Emerson pioneered the transcendentalist movement through a series of lectures. One of his most famed orations, "The American Scholar," was delivered on August 31, 1837, at Harvard's Phi Beta Kappa Day. He closed with these words: "We will walk on our own feet; we will work with our own hands; we will speak our own minds." Emerson continued writing and lecturing until his death on April 27, 1882, in Concord, Massachusetts.

—Melissa A. Chronister

A Gracious Friend

Alfred McAdam

Thank you, God, for giving me
    A faithful friend or two
Who reflect the lovely graces that
    Are such a part of You.
They so inspire and stimulate
    The inner core of me.
I am aspiring now, dear Lord,
    To follow close to Thee.

Such friends as these who see the good
    And know the other part
Have gradually entwined themselves
    About my very heart
And made of every moment lived
    A carrier of peace,
Where tensions caused by fear and doubt
    Can find supreme release.

O Lord, I wish that You would make
    Of me a gracious friend
Upon whose loyalty and love
    Another can depend.
Whose understanding heart would help
    Another man to be
Emulating more and more
    The qualities of Thee.

THE CHESS GAME
Alice Kent Stoddard, artist (1884–1976)
David David Gallery, Philadelphia
Superstock

BITS & PIECES

*F*riendships form among people who strengthen one another.
—*Franklin Owen*

A friend is someone with whom
you dare to be yourself.
—*C. Raymond Beran*

*O*ld friends, old scenes will lovelier be
As more of heav'n in each we see.
—*John Keble*

*F*riendship without self-interest
is rare and beautiful.
—*James Francis Byrnes*

*R*are as is true love, true
friendship is still rarer.
—*François,
Duc de La Rochefoucauld*

*T*he happiest miser on earth is the man
who saves up every friend he can make.
—*Robert Emmet Sherwood*

*M*y friend peers in on me with merry
Wise face, and though the sky stays dim,
The very light of day, the very
Sun's self comes in with him.
—*Algernon Charles Swinburne*

*F*riends who understand each other speak
with words sweet and strong which emerge
from their hearts like the fragrance of orchids.
—*Confucius*

What's a Greeting Card?

Author Unknown

It's a little piece of paper
That tells someone how you care.
It can be a ray of sunshine;
It can be a wish or prayer.

It can simply say "I love you"
Or just say "I understand."
It can be a little visit
Or the clasp of someone's hand.

It can be a word of comfort
When somebody's heart is sad;
It can be a smile or chuckle
Making someone's heart feel glad.

It can keep folks close together
Even though they're far apart;
It can show someone you're thankful
From the bottom of your heart.

It can travel any distance,
In all kinds of weather, too.
And it has the magic something
That some big things never do.

Yes, it's just a piece of paper,
And it costs no big amount,
But it proves that old, old saying:
"It's the little things that count."

A Special Greeting

Gladys Shuman

To send a friendly greeting
Is more than just a trend.
It's a habit I've established
Like chatting with a friend!
For even though we're miles apart,
I've wished the miles away;
So it's like a pleasant visit
To send a card your way!

WRITING TO A FRIEND
Al Riccio Photography

DON'T GROW AWAY

Douglas Malloch

Don't grow away from things of old,
    From things of old too fast;
So many change love's honest gold
    For coin that will not last.
Perhaps you once were ragged clad,
    And now that rich you are;
But from the things that once you had
    Don't grow away too far.

Don't grow away from older friends
    Because you have the new;
A man has many when he spends,
    In poverty a few,
And you may find, you yet may learn,
    The old are all that stay;
You yet may long to them to turn—
    Don't grow too far away.

Whatever fortune may befall,
    Whatever friends you know,
The dearest memory, after all,
    Is that of long ago.
The time may come you long to roam
    To where the old things are,
The simple tastes, the humble home—
    Don't grow away too far.

Readers' Reflections

Editor's Note: Readers are invited to submit unpublished, original poetry for possible publication in future issues of Ideals. *Please send typed copies only; manuscripts will not be returned. Writers receive $10 for each published submission. Send material to Readers' Reflections, Ideals Publications Inc., 535 Metroplex Drive, Suite 250, Nashville, Tennessee 37211.*

KINDNESS AND FRIENDSHIP

Scatter your seeds of kindness
All enriching as you go.
Trust the harvest giver;
He will make each seed to grow.
Then until the happy end
Your life shall never lack a friend.

Just as the lovely flowers
Lend their sweetness to each day,
May we touch the lives of those we meet
In a kind and gentle way.

Viola Weber
Floradale, Ontario

A POCKET FULL OF SMILES

A message from a relative,
A phone call or a note;
How blest to hear a loved one's voice
Or read a line he wrote.

It's good to know what's happening
To the ones we hold most dear;
It almost makes us feel as though
They're somehow very near.

The special way they relate to us
Across the distant miles

Brings a warm and cozy feeling
And a pocket full of smiles.

I've an attic full of letters
I've collected through the years
That chronicle our family times,
The laughter and the tears.

No matter how far away we go,
Or whatever words have been said,
Our letters and correspondence will lead
Us back to the old homestead.

Pam Iseley
Greensboro, North Carolina

FRIENDSHIP

Friendship is a hug,
Friendship is a tear,
Friendship holds your hand
And makes it very clear
Whatever path you take,
Whatever comes your way,

Friendship gives you strength
To face each coming day.
Friendship is forever
And never will depart;
For the spirit of a friendship
Lives within the heart.

Diana Meschberger
Auburn, Indiana

FRIENDSHIP'S HAVEN
for Fran

The shelter of your friendship—
What a special place to be.
It takes my sad and gloomy days
And makes them bright for me.

The shelter of your friendship
Has erased so many fears
And given me the strength to fight
My battles through the years.

The shelter of your friendship
Shows me laughter, sometimes tears.
Yet there's always understanding,
For you listen and you hear.

The shelter of your friendship
Has been faithful and so true.
I bless the day you said, "Come in,"
For just inside was you.

The shelter of your friendship
Will endure the sands of time.
As the door stands ever open
So my love will, friend of mine.

Dema Opal Draper Matteson
Three Rivers, Michigan

MY LORD AND I

My Lord and I
Walk down the road,
And, side by side,
We share the load.

He understands
If I should cry;
We're more than friends,
My Lord and I.

He lights the way
When it grows dark
Until it's day
Within my heart.

He claps His hands
If I should smile;
We're more than friends,
My Lord and I.

Pat Mallory
Tyler, Texas

The Touch of Human Hands

Thomas Curtis Clark

The touch of human hands—
That is the boon we ask;
For groping, day by day,
Along the stony way,
We need the comrade heart
That understands
And the warmth, the living warmth
Of human hands.

The touch of human hands—
Not vain, unthinking words,
Nor that cold charity
Which shuns our misery;
We seek a loyal friend
Who understands
And the warmth, the loving warmth
Of human hands.

The touch of human hands—
Such care as was in Him
Who walked in Galilee
Beside the silver sea;
We need a patient guide
Who understands
And the warmth, the pulsing warmth
Of human hands.

THROUGH MY WINDOW

Pamela Kennedy

Art by Ron Adair

MY MOTHER, MY DAUGHTER, MY FRIEND

As an only child, I spent lots of time with my mother. She was there in the morning when I awoke and regularly tucked me in at night. In between we took walks, read books, played dolls, and talked about all kinds of things.

She taught me to ride a bike, swim, sew, and make pies. And in addition to all this, she demonstrated in large and small ways how to be caring and compassionate to others, how to be assertive without being obnoxious. She gave me confidence to be myself and the forgiveness I needed to grow from my mistakes. In short, she was, and still is, my good friend.

I have friends who do not get along with their mothers, and I pity them; for I have come to understand, from both sides, that there is a special friendship unique to the mother-daughter relationship. I must have somehow learned this at a very young age, for my mother recalls me telling her that someday I wanted to grow up and have a little girl who loved me like I loved her. In His perfect timing, God decided to allow me to experience two sons before bringing a beautiful daughter into our family.

My sons are young men now, and I think we are pretty good friends; but I know for sure we don't communicate the same way as my daughter and I do. For one thing, sons communicate in verbal shorthand.

"How was your day?" elicits one of the following comments:

"Okay."

"You don't want to know."

"Cool."

Or any undecipherable grunt or groan. My daughter, on the other hand, launches into a monologue detailing who said what to whom and the ensuing effects on herself and all others in the general vicinity. If I want details, I ask her. If I'm in a hurry, I ask the guys.

When I go shopping with my sons, I wear my track shoes and don't plan to run any extra errands. They go to the store with an objective: get the Super 1020 Turbo Car Stereo Amplifier. They are not interested in what's on sale in another department. They do not care about visiting other stores. They *do not* want to browse or, heaven forbid, window-shop!

My daughter and I, however, can spend an entire afternoon looking for the right pair of earrings and may take many detours through the lingerie department, the bookstore, and perhaps the pet shop (just to see if that adorable gray kitten is still there). Even if we do not find the earrings, we come home feeling satisfied. We had a fun afternoon together. We "shopped."

Although these two examples of the differences between my relationships with my sons and my daughter aren't exhaustive, I think they illustrate some of the characteristics that make mother-daughter friendships so rewarding. In a household where baseball stats, engine speeds, and fishing lures often dominate after-dinner conversation, it's nice to have someone to talk with about relationships and feelings. When I'm tired of action movies and invasions from outer space, it's good to see a romance with someone who appreciates the genteel manners of the nineteenth century and understands why I shed a tear when the young lovers finally discover their affection for one another. When I need an opinion on a hair style or clothing choice, I'm glad to have some elaboration beyond, "Okay, I guess. Do you know where I left my needle-nose pliers?" Perhaps it's due to some genetic gender code, maybe it's just feminine fluke; whatever causes it, I appreciate the benefits of having someone in the family who thinks like I do.

As my daughter enters adolescence, I gratefully see us developing the kind of friendship my mother and I share. Although we do not always have the same views on things, we respect and appreciate one another, and I look forward to a deepening and enduring relationship with her. It delights me to realize that my childhood wish has come true, for I know what a blessing it is to have a mother and daughter be best friends.

Pamela Kennedy is a freelance writer of short stories, articles, essays, and children's books. Wife of a naval officer and mother of three children, she has made her home on both U.S. coasts and currently resides in Honolulu, Hawaii. She draws her material from her own experiences and memories, adding highlights from her imagination to enhance the story.

Tapestry

Nancy Merical

We weave our cloth of life with threads
Of hours and days we're given
And make a pattern that reflects
The face of God in heaven.
He gives us days of greatest joy
That cast a lovely hue,
But days of sorrow we must bear
For darker colors too.
Some days have trials woven in
That give our cloth its strength,
So other days that are misused
Won't cause a tear or rent.
Friends add texture to our cloth
And shining highlights leave;
New ones silver, old ones gold
Affect the warp and weave.
Faith is the shuttle we employ
To weave a better cloth,
And love we use to weave it too;
Love makes it smooth and soft.
Some days we weave silken threads
And some days coarse and rough;
One day's threads are stout and strong,
Another's softest fluff.
But when our cloth of life is woven
And taken from the frame,
It is unique, one of a kind;
None other is the same.
For though the same days we are given,
We use them differently
And make a pattern all our own
In God's great tapestry.

BERLIN WOOLWORK PILLOW. Designed by Elizabeth Bradley Designs. Crafted by Patricia A. Pingry. Jerry Koser Photography.

BERLIN WOOLWORK PILLOW
Mary Skarmeas

I have, in the corner of my living room, nestled against the armrest of a favorite old rocking chair, a pillow given to me by one of my sisters, something she herself received from a dear old friend years ago. It is a beautiful square pillow covered entirely on one side with exquisitely detailed needlework depicting a group of richly colored flowers against a background of deep green and blues. I have always marvelled at this pillow, at the thousands of small stitches made in what must be the softest wool yarn I have ever felt, but I did not know until recently that this familiar old pillow is actually an example of a craft called Berlin woolwork.

A little research revealed that Berlin woolwork is centuries old. It had its origins in the churches of thirteenth century Europe. Churchwomen decorated seat covers and kneelers with cross-stitched wool on heavy canvas, a practice that was as practical as it was decorative. Not only did the wool on canvas—known as Cushion style—make worshippers more comfortable in their pews, it was also a durable combination. Cushion style, characterized by cross-stitching in wool over the entire surface of a piece of canvas, soon evolved beyond the church and became known more broadly as canvas work. The name *Berlin woolwork* took over in the early 1800s, when printsellers in Berlin began selling patterns for canvas work copied from famous paintings of the day. The patterns were hand-painted onto paper over a grid which indicated the number of stitches. Around the same time, the fine Merino wool produced in Berlin became the accepted favorite for this type of stitching, further cementing the association of the city of Berlin with this unique style of needlework.

The popularity of Berlin work reached its peak in the mid-nineteenth century. The number of different stitches used grew from the simple cross and tent stitches to a list that included back, satin, and tapestry stitches as well as such fancy stitches as damask, herringbone, Irish, leviathan, treble, raised, rep, and more. Patterns continued to be taken from paintings—landscapes, florals, figures, and more—and geometric patterns also had their run in popularity. In England, young Queen Victoria herself was fond of Berlin work; and she, Prince Albert, and their large family were even the subject of more than one Berlin work pattern. What was distinctive of all Berlin work was the fine wool yarn and the intricate detail of the stitching. Stitching Berlin work was much like completing a painting: every inch of the canvas was filled with color in infinite varieties and gradations.

My first impression of Berlin woolwork was that it was too intricate and challenging for a novice stitcher, but I have discovered that it is much like my own beloved craft of knitting. So often a non-knitter will gaze upon a project I have completed with wonder and awe. I always try to tell such admirers that knitting does not require any great needleworking skills or an abundance of creativity. Once a pattern and colors have been selected, knitting is for the most part a function of following the instructions; and most patterns are repetitive. That's what makes it such a soothing and relaxing pastime. Berlin work is similar. The end result is a breathtaking work of art, but one must only choose a pattern and follow the stitch-by-stitch grid to create this masterpiece on needlepoint canvas. Yes, Berlin work, like knitting, does take patience and perseverance, and practice will improve both one's feel for the needle and the consistency of the stitches; but anyone can pick up a pattern and a needle and begin a Berlin work project.

Berlin work is not as popular as it once was, although it has experienced a revival of sorts in recent years—part of a taste for all things Victorian. I found a handful of beautiful books on the topic, with instructions and patterns included for projects ranging from the basic pillows and wall hangings to seat covers, clothing, curtain ties, and even carpets. And Berlin work kits, with pattern and wool included, are also available. Especially lovely are the kits, like the summer flowers pillow pictured at left, by designer Elizabeth Bradley.

I have no idea who stitched the pillow in my living room. It is older than my own memory, older than my sister's memory; even her friend, who passed the pillow along many years ago, did not know the name of its creator or the date of its creation. But here it remains, its richly colored beauty adding a touch of character and grace to my living room. Something about the deep, warm colors, the intricate stitching, and the texture of the wool is at once distinctly old-fashioned and perfectly in sync with the atmosphere of homiress I love to cultivate. The pillow does not grab for attention, but its richness rewards those who stop for a closer look. I think I shall try Berlin woolwork. I love crafts with staying power, crafts that reward an investment of time and care with quiet and timeless beauty.

Mary Skarmeas lives in Danvers, Massachusetts, and has recently earned her bachelor's degree in English at Suffolk University. Mother of four and grandmother of three, Mary loves all crafts, especially knitting.

A Stitch of Blue

June Masters Bacher

When there is rain, my neighbor comes
    To while away the day;
And as we chat and mend we find
    Skies are no longer gray.

We share a cup of tea beside
    An understanding fire
That knows to glow in embered tones
    Or reach its arms up higher.

And when the rain has stepped aside,
    Our mending's finished too;
We've patched our lives together with
    A little stitch of blue.

Sometimes I wish that more of life
    Were built of rainy days
So I could take the gray away
    In little, friendly ways.

Ideals' Family Recipes

Favorite Recipes from the Ideals Family of Readers

Editor's Note: Please send us your best-loved recipes! Mail a typed copy of the recipe along with your name, address, and phone number to Ideals magazine, ATTN: Recipes, P.O. Box 305300, Nashville, Tennessee 37230. We will pay $10 for each recipe used. Recipes cannot be returned.

OATMEAL MUFFINS

In a large bowl, soak 1 cup rolled oats in 1 cup buttermilk for 30 minutes. Preheat oven to 350° F. In a medium bowl, sift together 1 cup all-purpose flour, 1 teaspoon baking powder, ½ teaspoon baking soda, ½ teaspoon ground cinnamon, and ½ teaspoon salt. Set aside. Add 1 beaten egg to oats mixture and mix well. Add ½ cup firmly packed brown sugar and ½ cup melted and cooled shortening. Stir in flour mixture. Stir in ½ cup raisins. Spoon batter into greased muffin cups. Bake 15 to 20 minutes. Makes 1 dozen muffins.

Mary A. Monnig
Glasgow, Missouri

PEANUT BUTTER MUFFINS

Preheat oven to 350° F. In a large bowl, sift together 2 cups all-purpose flour, ⅓ cup granulated sugar, 2 teaspoons baking powder, and 1 teaspoon salt. With a pastry blender or fork, cut in 1 cup chunky peanut butter until mixture is crumbly. Add 1 cup milk and 1 beaten egg; stir well. Spoon batter into greased muffin cups, filling each about ⅔ full. Bake 20 to 25 minutes or until tops begin to crack. Makes 12 muffins.

Lois Harvey
Winona, Minnesota

COFFEE SHOP CORN MUFFINS

Preheat oven to 425° F. In a large bowl, combine 1¼ cup corn meal, 1 cup all-purpose flour, ⅓ cup granulated sugar, ⅓ cup firmly packed brown sugar, 1 teaspoon baking soda, and ½ teaspoon salt. Set aside. In a medium bowl, combine 1 egg, 1 cup buttermilk, and ¾ cup vegetable oil; beat lightly. Add buttermilk mixture to flour mixture all at once; stir just until blended. Spoon batter into well-greased muffin cups, filling each about ⅔ full. Bake 15 to 20 minutes until golden brown and a toothpick inserted in the center comes out clean. Makes 12 to 14 muffins.

Clare Masyada
Woodbridge, New Jersey

BERRY MUFFINS

Preheat oven to 400° F. In a large bowl, sift together 1 cup whole wheat flour, ¾ cup all-purpose flour, ½ cup granulated sugar, 1 tablespoon baking powder, and ½ teaspoon salt. Stir in ¼ cup wheat germ; set aside. In a separate large bowl, combine 1 egg, 3 tablespoons vegetable oil, and 1 cup milk. Add flour mixture and stir well. Fold in 1 cup fresh blueberries or blackberries. Spoon batter into greased muffin cups, filling each about ⅔ full. Bake 20 to 25 minutes or until a toothpick inserted in the center comes out clean. Makes 12 to 14 muffins.

Barb Marshall
Pickerington, Ohio

BUTTERMILK BRAN MUFFINS

Preheat oven to 400° F. In a large bowl, sift together 1¼ cup all-purpose flour, ½ cup granulated sugar, 1¼ teaspoon baking soda, and ¼ teaspoon salt. Add 3 cups bran flakes; stir well. Set aside. In a small bowl, combine ¼ cup vegetable oil, 1 egg, and 1 cup buttermilk; beat until thoroughly blended. Add egg mixture to flour mixture and stir just until moistened. Spoon batter into greased muffin cups. Bake 12 to 15 minutes or until a toothpick inserted in the center comes out clean. Makes 16 muffins.

Mrs. Amos S. Eicher
Oconto, Wisconsin

Devotions FROM THE Heart

Pamela Kennedy

"A friend loveth at all times, and a brother is born for adversity."
Proverbs 17:17

A BLESSED FRIENDSHIP

I stood on the porch and waved good-bye as my friend, Linda, pulled out of the driveway. How I enjoyed her visits! As often as our busy schedules allowed, we carved out time to visit a local park, catch a bit of lunch, take in a movie, or just sit and talk at home. Together we shared ideas and experiences about decorating, dealing with our adult children, impending career changes, and family crises. We have always shared a comfortable, easy friendship devoid of competition or touchiness.

Too bad, I thought as I turned and went inside, that there aren't more friendships like ours. Some people seem to want to be friends only when things are going badly, or when they need something. Others want to be friends only when it's convenient, or until someone more exciting or interesting comes along. As I picked up the empty cups and rinsed the lunch dishes, I flipped on the radio to a favorite station and hummed along. I was replacing the dishes on the shelves when the words to the radio hymn penetrated my thoughts: "What a friend we have in Jesus. . . ."

It was an old and familiar sentiment. In fact, I recall my grandmother singing it when I was just a little girl. But because of my thoughts about my friendship with Linda, it was as if I heard the words for the first time. What struck me wasn't the realization of the Lord's friendship toward me, but of how I reciprocated that friendship. What kind of a friend was I to Him?

My prayertime usually consisted of a few introductory "thank yous" followed by a long litany of "pleases." Please help me get through this busy week. Please give me wisdom to know what to say. Please heal me of this illness quickly. Please watch over my loved ones. There was no time for listening, few questions that weren't related to my needs or wants. Somehow, in my relationship with my heavenly Father, I had become just the kind of friend I didn't like. When things were going well, I never stopped by for a chat. When the sun was shining, I was too busy for conversation. But let dark clouds gather at my horizon, let worry knock at my front door, and there I was on my knees asking for favors.

I know God wants us to come to Him with our problems and concerns. And I am certain He willingly helps us bear our burdens. But I wonder if He also longs for us to be close friends with Him, friends who can't wait to tell Him when something wonderful happens. Does His heart gladden when we pour out our joy to Him? As we marvel at a rainbow or a magnificent mountain or the delicate symmetry of a dragonfly, would He like to hear a word of appreciation? Is there a place in His heart that warms when we express our gratitude for the wonders of breath and heartbeat?

Near the end of His earthly life, when He spoke with His disciples, Jesus told them He would no longer call them servants but would call them His friends. Wasn't He telling us that too? He desires us to be friends who visit with Him at all times—friends who truly enjoy one another's company.

I turned off the radio and sat down at the kitchen table. I imagined Jesus sitting across from me, sharing a cup of coffee, spending time with me just like good friends do. A smile crept into the corners of my mouth as I recalled something Linda had shared. "Lord," I whispered softly, "wait till You hear what happened today."

Thank you, Lord, for being a friend who loves me at all times. Help me to demonstrate that
kind of friendship to You as well as to others.
AMEN.

Friendship

Carice Williams

How good it is to have a friend
    To share a joy or two
And better still to have a friend
    When one is feeling blue.
For friends are like the gentle flowers
    That bloom in gardens fair.
They yield a bounty of great joy
    If given love and care.

A Garden of Friends

June Masters Bacher

Open a packet of sunshine
    And sprinkle it on the wind;
It will go traveling widely
    And soon it will find a friend.
Open a packet of flowers
    That bloom wherever they blow
(Smiles and kind words are the sunshine
    They need to take root and grow).

Each friend will share with another
    A deed or so every day
Till sun and seed you have scattered
    Have formed a giant bouquet.

From My Garden Journal

by Deana Deck

GLOXINIA

I am a cut-flower fanatic. I love to have cut flowers in every room in my house, and I love to share them. Visitors invariably go home with fresh bouquets—from spring to autumn, from crocuses to chrysanthemums. Luckily, I live in a temperate climate, so I can share freshly cut flowers with friends well into autumn. But sooner or later, a hard freeze comes and puts an end to flowers in the house.

I make do for a while with dried hydrangeas or plumes from the pampas grass; and then, as we go into the holidays, I switch to masses of fresh holly. A white or pink poinsettia usually appears about mid-December and will get me as far into the next year as mid-January. But soon the last poinsettia leaf has fallen, and I turn to flowering houseplants to add color to my home. The gloxinia remains one of my favorites. It responds well to artificial light and can be encouraged to start blooming indoors in the middle of winter. The gloxinia's huge, velvety leaves and brilliantly colored, tubular blooms banish the gray-day gloom from my corner of the world. The plant doubles for freshly cut flowers in another important way: sharing with friends is a snap!

The gloxinia is a *gesneriad*, a member of the same family as the African violet. There's a mystery of sorts here. If you look up gloxinia in the index of any flowering houseplant book, it will invariably refer you to "sinningia hybrids." Every reference to gloxinia that I found points out the fact that the plant *used* to be known as the gloxinia, but now both *sinningia* and *gloxinia* are used interchangeably.

Of the two popular varieties of gloxinia, the one most commonly available is a modern form of *Sinningia speciosa*, a tuberous-rooted Brazilian wildflower. The blooms may be white, pink, red, lavender, or purple, often with contrasting edges or spots of a different hue. The furry leaves form a compact base for the blooms that cluster above them. The other variety is the *Sinningia pusilla*, sometimes referred to as a miniature gloxinia because of its dainty, half-inch, purple blooms.

One reason I like these charming plants is because they are so easy to share with friends. If a visitor admires a particular specimen, you can snip off a leaf for her, drop it into a plastic bag, and send it on its way to a new home. You can even put snipped leaves in the mail!

The best way to start a new plant is to fill a six-inch pot with rich, damp potting soil. Leave a small, cup-shaped

GLOXINIA

hollow in the center of the potting soil and fill it with a rooting medium such as vermiculite, perlite, or even a half and half mixture of coarse sand and damp peat moss. Think of the hollow as a little island in a sea of potting mix.

Using a razor blade or a sharp knife, cut a medium-sized, healthy leaf from the gloxinia. Make the cut about two inches below the base of the leaf. Dip this leaf tip into rooting hormone and then insert it into the little island of rooting medium in the center of the pot. Set the leaf in at a slight angle, so that when a new plantlet appears at its base, the leaf won't block the light. The rooting medium will provide an ideal environment for the leaf to root in; and as the plant begins to mature and requires more nutrients, the roots will be able to reach beyond the rooting medium into the richer potting soil.

Cover the pot with a plastic bag, using drinking straws, chopsticks, or stakes to support it and form a small greenhouse. Place the pot in bright, indirect light and keep the temperature between 50° F and 70° F. Do not add water unless the plastic bag appears dry. In ideal conditions, the bag will exhibit a fine layer of moisture. If large droplets start running down the bag, open the bag to let some of the excess moisture escape.

In two to three weeks, you can start looking for shoots to appear. Once new shoots have appeared, open the bag but leave it in place for about three days to acclimate the plant. Then remove the bag and treat it like any other gloxinia. (Keep in bright, curtain-filtered light. Water from the bottom, and avoid splashing the leaves. Keep the soil moist but not too wet or the roots will rot. Feed monthly while growing; African violet food is ideal.)

This method of propagation is excellent for rooting a single cutting because once the shoots have appeared, it will not be necessary to repot the new plant. If you want several new plants, however, you can root several leaves in a single container of rooting medium, then transplant the new shoots to individual pots when they are about one-third the size of the parent leaf.

The only frustrating characteristic of gloxinia plants is that they bloom once and then go dormant; unlike their cousin, the miniature gloxinia, which, like the African violet, will bloom year round with the right amount of light, food, and water.

When your gloxinia is going dormant, it will cease blooming and the leaves will start turning yellow. At this point, stop feeding it and begin to gradually reduce watering. By the time the leaves shrivel and drop off, you should not be watering the plant at all.

Put the pot in the basement or a similar dry, frost-free area for two to four months. All on its own the plant will start growing again. As soon as you spot the first tender shoots, move it back into the light and resume normal care.

Now when my friends stop by for a visit by the fire during these chilly days of late autumn, I present them with a cheery gloxinia that I've started from a single leaf. The gloxinia has saved my reputation among my friends for always having a gift for them from my garden. But in this case, the garden is my indoor garden of houseplants!

Deana Deck tends to her flowers, plants, and vegetables at her home in Nashville, Tennessee, where her popular garden column is a regular feature in The Tennessean.

FOR THE CHILDREN

MY DOG
Marchette Chute

His nose is short and scrubby;
His ears hang rather low;
And he always brings the stick back,
No matter how far you throw.

He gets spanked rather often
For things he shouldn't do,
Like lying-on-beds and barking
And eating up shoes when they're new.

He always wants to be going
Where he isn't supposed to go.
He tracks up the house when it's snowing—
Oh, puppy, I love you so.

CURIOUS KITTENS. Dick Dietrich Photography.

A Common Calling

Margaret Rorke

I heard her calling "Mildred"
In accents loud and clear,
This not too distant neighbor;
But Mildred didn't hear.
Again the name repeated,
More urgent than before;
But when there was no answer,
I heard her voice implore,
"Here! Kitty, kitty, kitty!"

Then came a little tinkle
Across the nearby street.
I judged that it was Mildred
On four a-flying feet.
There's something 'bout the rhythm,
Regardless of the name,
One universal summons
Invites all cats the same:
"Here! Kitty, kitty, kitty!"

50

Playmates

Mary Ellen Stelling

What a life our puppy leads
Filling his small owners' needs!
First he's wearing dolly clothes,
Then sporting specs upon his nose.
They fence him in with rocking chairs
And make him kneel to say his prayers;
They tie blue ribbons on his tail
Or make believe that he's in jail.
They put some booties on his feet
And serve him muddy pies to eat.
And through it all, he wags and licks
The little hands which play these tricks!

SHAR-PEI PUPPY. Dick Dietrich Photography.

Back to School

Craig E. Sathoff

It's back to class and back to books
    For all the girls and boys
Who merrily skip toward the school
    With mingled woe and joy.

It's apple-for-the-teacher time—
    The end of summer play.
It's hit-the-books-with-vigor time;
    It's study hard each day.

It's quite a new experience
    For the little bright-eyed girl
Who starts to kindergarten class,
    Her young mind in a whirl.

And it is such a pensive day
    For Mother home alone,
Who finds the house too quiet now
    With all her children gone.

It's time to guide and shape each child
    That he may serve to be
An asset to his inner self
    And his community.

Remember When

THE WALK TO SCHOOL

Marjorie Holmes

I have always felt sorry for children who miss the experience of walking to school.

When I was a small town youngster we walked at least a mile each way, whatever the weather. And the distance was fraught with wonder, no matter how familiar its landmarks became.

On certain corners there were magic talismans to be invoked—simple lettering on the sidewalk immortalizing some builder's name. Yet the first one to stamp on them and shout, "Good luck!" was sure to be protected from evil all day.

And there were houses that loomed with significance en route. There was the Flower Lady whose entire yard was a riot of blossoms and who might give you some for teacher if she felt in a generous mood . . .

There was the sheriff's house; he could arrest you and throw you in jail if he chose, the older kids claimed . . . There was the Witch's House, an ancient red brick with cupolas and towers, where a daft old lady lived; she sometimes sang from a window, or scurried out in her little white cap to ask if you'd seen her angels who'd flown off again.

There was the Presbyterian Church with its mighty chimes and clock, and its bubbling drinking fountain . . . There was that whispering treasure house, the public library. On the way home you could stop and borrow

exactly two books, no more. But by starting them as you sauntered along, you could have them read by tomorrow and borrow two more.

In the fall there was the scent of apple orchards and the dusty scuff and rattle of fallen leaves. You picked up the loveliest samples, scarlet maple, golden beech, to show your teacher, then pin on a paper to trace.

When the first snow fell, you raced joyously through it, trying to catch the cool lacy flakes on your tongue. Drifts did not deter you. They were an excuse to wade.

Snow and ice held the earth fast most of winter, followed by a miracle when the warm days came. For now the gutters ran wild with the melted waters, and sidewalks mirrored an upside-down world of sky and clouds and trees. And gazing down, down, you felt a breathless transporting.

You were one of the five foolish princesses
who ran off
at night into
the world beneath
the world and danced
their slippers to shreds.

You spied the first robin on your way to school. And the first crocus, and it was news. And there were seedpods to be stepped on; how they squirted. And the fuzz of cottonwoods to catch, and dandelion fluff to be blown. And violets to be gathered in a shady wood, and clover to be braided. And you bounced balls, skipped ropes, and raced to join friends who were waiting, or they rushed up to join you. And you argued and philosophized and giggled and dreamed big dreams as you made this daily pilgrimage.

There was time for these things, to think and wonder and truly be a child on these long walks to school.

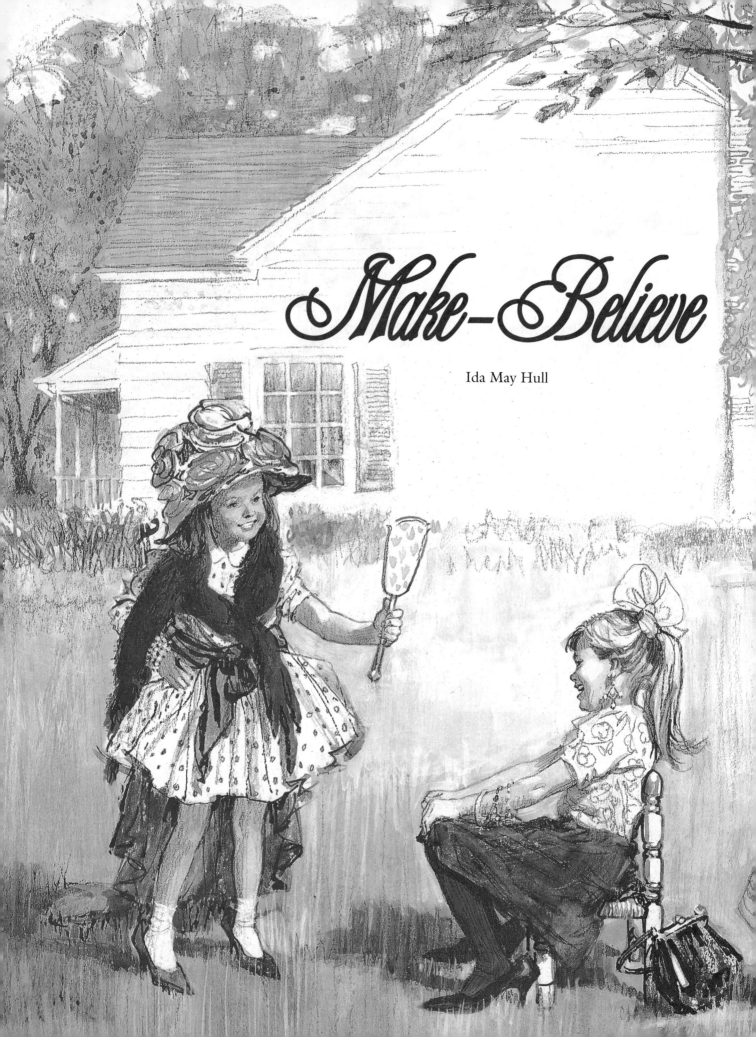

Make-Believe

Ida May Hull

Two little girls in trailing dresses,
Hair coiled back in lustrous tresses,
Spike heels clicking down the walk,
Are busy making "grown-up" talk.

With flowered hats and smiling faces,
They flaunt their girlish charms and graces.
Wondering eyes light up and shine;
In make-believe, they dance and dine.

Tired from their play, two little misses
Come to me for good-night kisses,
Cuddle up within my arms,
And woo me with their girlish charms.

A SLICE OF LIFE

Edgar A. Guest

THE FELLOWSHIP OF BOOKS

I care not who the man may be,
    Nor how his tasks may fret him,
Nor where he fares, nor how his cares
    And troubles may beset him,
If books have won the love of him,
    Whatever fortune hands him,
He'll always own, when he's alone,
    A friend who understands him.

Though other friends may come and go,
    And some may stoop to treason,
His books remain, through loss or gain,
    And season after season

The faithful friends for every mood,
    His joy and sorrow sharing,
For old time's sake, they'll lighter make
    The burdens he is bearing.

Oh, he has counsel at his side,
    And wisdom for his duty,
And laughter gay for hours of play,
    And tenderness and beauty,
And fellowship divinely rare,
    True friends who never doubt him,
Unchanging love, and God above,
    Who keeps good books about him.

Edgar A. Guest began his illustrious career in 1895 at the age of fourteen when his work first appeared in the Detroit Free Press. His column was syndicated in over three hundred newspapers, and he became known as "The Poet of the People."

Patrick McRae is an artist who lives in the Milwaukee, Wisconsin, area. He has created nostalgic artwork for Ideals for more than a decade, and his favorite models are his wife and three children.

Old Things

Edna Jaques

I love old things, old books, old friends,
The lovely way an old tree bends
Above a little clapboard house,
A tiny yard still as a mouse.

A zig-zag fence of cedar rails,
A stout old ship with mended sails,
Tall trees around a village square,
A chest of thin, old silverware.

An old log house beyond the town,
Its oaken rafters falling down
Yet holding in each chimney stone,
An ageless beauty of its own.

I love the sheen of oaken floors,
Wrought iron hinges on old doors,
The sound that flowing water makes,
The weathered brown of cedar shakes.

I love old things . . . timeworn and frayed,
Upon whose heart the years have laid
A kindly touch as if to show
The beauty of their inner glow.

Collectors

Vera B. Hammann

Some folks collect antiques galore,
While some buy bells with ancient lore;
And others treasure rings and pins,
Or cookie cutters made of tin;
While some pour over books of stamps,
Or pictures of old baseball champs.
A few prefer folk songs of old,
And others coins and dust of gold.
Then china with a history
For others holds a mystery.
Old clocks and watches, any kind,
No matter if the stems don't wind,
Are cherished as real old heirlooms
Displayed in cases built in rooms.
Collectors are an earnest group,
And in antique shops love to snoop;
But as for me, my heart contends
'Tis better to collect good friends!

The Fireplace

Roger W. Dana

There's nothing like a fireplace,
    So quaint and cozy warm,
A place of solid comfort
    And of refuge from life's storm;
A place for friends to gather
    And of old times reminisce;
Or where a blushing boy and girl
    Perhaps could steal a kiss.
A place to tell fish stories,
    Some quite true and some quite tall,
With bright and cheery fire
    Casting shadows on the wall;
To have life's cares forgotten
    With its mad and hurried pace;
To rest and let the world go by
    Just try a fireplace.

STONE FIREPLACE IN A LOG CABIN
Jessie Walker Associates

CORNER

CUCKOO CLOCKS

by Lisa C. Ragan

My fascination with cuckoo clocks began when I was a small child visiting my aunt Shirley in Kentucky. Aunt Shirley had traveled all over the world and had collected many interesting items from her journeys, but the one that captured my attention most was her cuckoo clock. Aunt Shirley bought the clock when she was traveling through the Black Forest region of Germany. It looked to me like a miniature mountain cabin decorated with dark leaves and birds. I felt a surge of excitement every hour when that mysterious bird would spring from its home in the wooden clock and sound its two-note greeting above the din of whirring and chiming which always accompanied it. I wanted to follow the cuckoo back into its quiet home to see what it looked like in there. Because Aunt Shirley always remembered how I loved the cuckoo clock, she passed it on to me when she died. Aunt Shirley's clock is my favorite clock in my collection. Her clock is not only the reason I began collecting cuckoo clocks, but it also serves as an hourly reminder of a special aunt's love.

While I am fond of and include in my collection the most popular style of cuckoo clock with its dark wood, carved leaves, and weights in the shape of fir cones, my preference in style is that of an earlier cuckoo clock, of which I have only one. Its shape resembles the traditional Black Forest wall clock with the addition of a little door from which the cuckoo joyfully emerges every hour. A simpler style, this clock is in the shape of a rectangle with a semicircle above it. The face and house are a soft cream color with hand-painted flowers around the face and the cuckoo's door.

I discovered this early clock while visiting the little town in Kentucky where my mother and aunt both grew up. I was rummaging through a junk store on the outskirts of town. This was one of those shops where most of what you see is fodder for the neighborhood garage sale, but every now and then an authentic antique of remarkable quality calls to you from a dusty corner. This lovely clock, chipped and scratched though it is, was shoved back on a bottom shelf with several old radios. I bought it quickly and without haggling too much over the price and took it to a clock repair shop for a tune-up. It works surprisingly well for its age, which is approximately one hundred and fifty years. As the prized piece in my collection, this clock hangs in a place of honor above my fireplace mantel.

My collection of cuckoo clocks numbers only ten, but each clock means something special to me. The clocks hang in every room of my house and cause quite a ruckus on the hour. I have become so accustomed to the sound that I sleep undisturbed every night, but the cacophony can be quite jolting to my guests. When company comes to visit, I usually quiet my clocks for the night.

While I have gleaned my collection thus far from antique galleries, estate sales, and even junk stores, all on American soil, I hope to travel to Germany some day to add to my collection. The cost of traveling there doesn't threaten my pocketbook nearly as much as does the thought of buying up every cuckoo clock I see!

TIMELY INFORMATION

If you would like to start a collection of cuckoo clocks, here are some interesting facts:

HISTORY

• While often mistakenly associated with Switzerland, the cuckoo clock actually originated in the Black Forest region of Germany and dates back to about 1730.

• Credit for inventing the cuckoo clock is generally given to Franz Anton Ketterer of Schönwald.

• After 1780, wooden wheel mechanisms in clocks were gradually replaced with brass as brass-casting was introduced to the region.

CUCKOO CLOCK DESIGNS

• Cuckoo clocks are made from wood available from trees in the Black Forest region of Germany, primarily mahogany, lime, or oak.

• Early cuckoo clock designs mimicked the popular designs of other Black Forest clocks—which had wooden dials covered with paper—but added a small door from which the cuckoo would emerge. As the cuckoo clock's popularity increased, later designs featured painted and varnished dials.

• By 1870, the most popular cuckoo clock design was introduced—a small, wooden house adorned with carved wooden leaves and/or animals and white, carved Gothic numerals and hands (usually made out of bone or horn) on a dark face.

• The most popular carvings on the cuckoo clocks are:
  • leaves
  • rabbits
  • deer
  • birds, particularly the cuckoo

• Sometimes a second door was added to the clock from which emerged a one-note quail to sound the time at every quarter of an hour.

CUCKOO CLOCKS. Unicorn Stock Photos.

FOCUSING YOUR COLLECTION

Due to the wide variety of cuckoo clocks, many collectors narrow their searches to one category. For example:

• The most famous makers of cuckoo clocks were several members of the Kammerer family and Johann Baptist Beha of Eisenbach.

• The trumpeter clock was introduced in 1857 by Jakob Bäuerle in Furtwangen. It featured a tiny, carved man, usually in the form of a soldier, who came out of the miniscule doors to sound the hour. Few trumpeter clocks were manufactured.

• Collectors might choose to concentrate on particular styles, such as painted dials, wooden carvings, or clocks which feature a particular animal.

INSCRIPTION
for a Birdhouse

Gail Brook Burket

Blessed be each welcome, feathered guest
These walls will shelter well and long.
May happiness attend your flights
And fill your hearts and throats with song.

We love the lilting gaiety
Of morning trills and lively wings.
This tiny haven says small thanks
For half the joy your coming brings.

Bird Thoughts
While Raking

Grace Cornell Tall

Leaves of all colors
Spin from the trees.
Oh, where are the birds
With a liking for these?
Birds take every cherry
And berry they find,
And I've never objected
Or pretended I mind.
Now I am willing
To give them a share

Of the leaves that are spilling
Pell-mell down the air
And weaving a carpet
So lush and so high
Not a blade of green grass
Gets a glimpse of the sky.
I have raked into piles
Leaves up to my knees,
Which the night winds will chase
And disperse as they please.

Are there not *any* birds
Who will help me with these?
Come, birds, like the leaf-bearing
Dove of the ark, and carry away
These leaves after dark.
O birds, be my friends,
For it's wind against rake—
What flies from the piles
After dark,
Come and take!

66

Autumn in a Glass

Betty Cornwell

I caught autumn
In a glass—
Scarlet leaf;
Saffron grass.

Goldenrod and
Purple vine;
Subdued perhaps,
But no less mine!

Autumn Light

Stella Craft Tremble

In autumn radiance strange and bright,
   The flowers glow with eerie light—
On lily pad and maple leaf,
   No drop of dew or rain-relief.

But haloes on all forms of life
   Vibrate in heat waves like a knife,
Dissolving things in burning light
   With golden glare that dims the sight.

Oh, may a cooler world unfold
   On glittering plots of marigold—
And rains of mercy fall in showers
   To bless with peace this world of ours.

MORNING IN THE COUNTRY
East Andover, New Hampshire
William Johnson/Johnson's Photography

Invitation
TO A GARDEN

Rose Koralewsky

The garden gate stands open wide
    To you who pass this way.
    Enter, for here is paradise
    This sunny autumn day.

Broad pools of mellow amber light
    Dapple the velvet grass,
    The zinnias and marigolds
    A glowing, tangled mass.

Above a rambling, low stone wall
    Pink spider lilies rise;

Cosmos in wine and white and rose
    Hover like butterflies.

Wee thistle birds in dipping flight
    Skim joyously along,
    Small golden punctuation marks
    In sentences of song.

A haunt of peace and loveliness,
    High-canopied with blue.
    Weaving a web of dreams untold,
    The garden waits for you.

Country CHRONICLE

—Lansing Christman—

SERENITY

I have a friendship with all four seasons of the year, and now I welcome autumn to my door. As I head out for my evening walk in the country, evidence of the season's majestic arrival fills my senses.

I can see autumn in the quickening evening hours. Days are getting shorter; and the lengthening shadows of trees, houses, barns, and sheds stretch across my path. The colors of the landscape are beginning to change to fall's magnificent palette, and the green leaves are surrendering to the reds and scarlets, golds and oranges of the coming season. From my path, I see the blossoms of the goldenrod, asters, and morning-glories, the ripening berries of the dogwood and bittersweet, and the woodbine and ivy.

I hear autumn's mellow chords marking the season's change. During the later days of summer, the birds are quiet. But as I walk beneath a grove of trees, I am pleased to hear again the robin's carol, the *o-ka-lee* of the redwing, and the warble of the bluebirds as they inspect their old nesting sites. A chorus of crickets fills the dooryards, gardens, and fields; and their chirping is joined by the chattering of chipmunks and squirrels as they busily prepare for approaching winter.

Once I leave the shelter of the woods, the crispness in the air reminds me that the nights will soon be cooler and more restful, and the myriad stars will shine all the brighter next to a golden harvest moon. Mornings will soon become sharp and clear, except for the bluish haze of Indian Summer that slips like a veil down the mountainsides to cover the faces of God's valleys and hills.

All around me, I witness the year entering its final phase in an aura of serenity. The beautiful colors and sounds of the coming season are symbols of the year's maturity, symbols of growing old with dignity and grandeur.

The author of two published books, Lansing Christman has been contributing to Ideals *for more than twenty years. Mr. Christman has also been published in several American, foreign, and braille anthologies. He lives in rural South Carolina.*

BUTTERFLY ON PURPLE CONEFLOWER. D. Petku/H. Armstrong Roberts.

September Days

Mina Morris Scott

BUTTERFLY ON FOLIAGE. Victoria, Canada. Dennis Frates/Oregon Scenics.

Sunny days of blue and gold,
    Long and languorous hours,
Soft, caressing breezes
    Scented by the flowers,
Now with harvest promised,
    Naught to do but rest;
After summer's labor,
    September days are best.

Whisper of the trembling leaves,
    Rhythm of the rain,
Cadences of songbirds
    Crooning a refrain,

Nights lit by the golden lamp
    Of harvest moon above,
Of all the autumn season
    These are the days I love.

The cricket and the katydid
    Sound their serenades;
Quacking wildfowl flutter
    In marshy esplanades;
In such lovely language,
    As benisons increase,
September writes her poem
    Of serenity and peace.

Upon a Rock

Anna M. Priestley

I wandered in the cloistered haunts
    Of shy, wild things,
Where gentle gossiping of trees
    And whir of wings
Were mingled with the elfin sound
    Made by the brook,
Where cricket orchestras struck up
    In every nook.

Then suddenly I came upon
    An ancient wall
Where ivy torches had been lit
    By passing fall;
Where grapevines counted purple beads
    The livelong day
And lichens spread their tapestries
    Of softest gray.

Men laid these stones for permanence,
    Without a thought
Of all the delicate designs
    The years have wrought.
They made a wall to stand a flood
    Or earthquake shock;
Now beauty builds her fragile house
    Upon that rock.

My Favorite Memory

Personal Stories of Treasured Memories from the Ideals Family of Readers

An Autumn Memory

The fragrant, leafy scents of autumn carried on familiar breezes remind me of when my family lived across the lane from my aunt, uncle, and cousins. As children, my cousins and I played together constantly through all seasons and all weather. The whole world was our two yards connected by a narrow, muddy lane that continued on to places we had yet to discover.

Fresh autumn days would find us dressed in bulky sweaters and hats that covered our ears. We spent so much of our time playing outdoors—tag, hide-and-seek, pretend games of house and school. Bedtime, bringing our days to a close, usually came soon after supper when light was fading and darkness beginning. But there was one exception.

Every fall, a day was set aside for yard cleanup. Work would begin in the afternoon, and we all helped. Toys were picked up, some to be put away and not seen again until next spring. Everyone raked, shoveled, and piled until both yards, including the lane, glistened with neatness and organization. One lonely pile of leaves, grass, twigs, and old sticks remained in the center of my cousins' yard where it caused great excitement and anticipation. Later in the evening, this pile of fall scrapings would become our bonfire.

Once supper was finished, when it seemed too dark for us to be out, we gathered again outside. We encircled the pile and waited for one of our parents to start the fire. A tiny puff of sweet smoke and small, flickering flame soon grew into a wonderful, bright blaze of crackling twigs and flying sparks. The fire's heat, the stinging smoke, and the quiet murmur of our parents' voices joined with our laughter to create a magic, perfect memory. As the fire died, we put small garden potatoes on top of the glowing coals. We roasted them until they were black and crunchy outside and soft and sweet inside. What a treat! What an evening!

I'm sure that later we were asleep as soon as our heads touched our pillows. Fall had been officially and ceremoniously brought to a close. We would now wait for winter's arrival, bringing with it opportunities for new adventures.

Marylyn Jessie
Terrace Bay, Ontario

My First Day of School

One September day in 1928, the neighbor children came by to take me to my first day at the country school a mile down the road. As I clutched my new pencil box and my red tin lunchbox, my five-year-old mind filled with dread of the unknown terrors that lay ahead. Mother gave me a hug, and I was on my way, turning repeatedly to wave one more time.

We arrived at the schoolyard just as the bell was ringing, and my companions took off for the schoolhouse. I followed until I came to the front steps. Then I stopped, afraid to go any farther. The sound of a familiar voice rescued me. "Come on in," urged my cousin Carol. "This is our teacher," she continued as I looked up into bright brown eyes peering from behind silver-rimmed glasses perched on a long, narrow nose. Mrs. Kissinger smiled, and her stern face became a welcoming one.

Mrs. Kissinger showed me where to leave my lunchbox in the cloakroom and took me to the front row of desks. I was given my own desk with a place for pencils, crayons, and a tablet. I listened with interest to the older children as each class was called to the recitation bench. I even liked the sound of the chalk scratching and screeching on the blackboard, and the smell of the chalk dust from the erasers.

At lunchtime, I sat with Carol on the steps of the schoolhouse to eat. I opened my new lunchbox to find a peanut butter and brown sugar sandwich, black walnut cake, and an apple from our orchard, polished until it shone.

I was too timid to join in any of the games or answer the teacher's questions, but when it was time to go home, I could hardly wait to share the exciting moments of my first day of school.

Betty Baldwin
Forest City, Iowa

A Place by the Sea

Set upon a small hill overlooking Buzzards Bay in Onset, Massachusetts, was a quaint home where I spent glorious days and tranquil evenings as a child. The house at 32 East Boulevard was built sometime in the late 1800s, and the sea air and wind had taken its toll. The white paint was peeling, and one of the red shutters was loose; but the wear and tear only added to the charm of the estate. The house belonged to my dearest friend Tania's grandparents, and I often accompanied her there for memorable visits. To me, this house by the sea was a special place where best friends shared secrets, laughter, and tears.

There was never a dull moment at 32 East Boulevard. This was mostly because Tania had three sisters and one brother. We all had a lot of common interests, due to our ages being so close together. Naturally, we had our share of quarrels, as all children do, but the good times we shared far outweighed the bad.

It seems as though something delicious was always coming out of the oven at "Grampa's" house. I can still recall the aroma of garlic roasted lamb filling the entire house. Cooking dinner was always Grampa's job, which left Gramma plenty of time to make her specialty— blueberry buckle. Gramma would put so many blueberries in the buckle that by the time we were finished eating, all of our tongues would be stained from the sweet, tiny fruit.

Our days were usually spent on the beach across from the house. We would spend endless hours creating elaborate sand castles and collecting stones and seashells. One of our favorite pastimes was digging for clams. We would fill our buckets with these creatures until our buckets were overflowing and almost too heavy to carry. I can still remember the big smile on Grampa's face when he would see us approaching him with all the shellfish. He always said that nothing tasted better on a sunny afternoon than steamed clams and drawn butter.

After a long day in the sun, there was something extremely comforting about coming home to Grampa's house. The bedroom that Tania and I shared was enormous. The walls were painted mint green and the doors and trim were painted white. The ceilings seemed tremendously high, and the windows were so oversized that the sills were only about one foot from the floor. French doors opened onto a spacious, glassed-in porch that was filled with white wicker furniture and overlooked the bay. Tania and I would sit in the wicker rocking chairs for hours, sharing our hopes, dreams, and fears.

Those nights were so peaceful; all that could be heard were the sounds of the leaves rustling in the wind, the rippling tide splashing on the shore, and the occasional hoot from the neighborhood owl. Sometimes in my mind I go back to that house to remember the carefree days of my childhood, dear friends, and a special place by the sea.

Maria Garland
Wakefield, Massachusetts

Editor's Note: Do you have a holiday or seasonal memory that you'd like to share with the Ideals family of readers? Send your typed memory to:

My Favorite Memory
c/o Editorial Department
Ideals Magazine
535 Metroplex Drive, Suite 250
Nashville, Tennessee 37211

OLD AGE

Tim Marks

The maples are burning,
Kindled with a silent flame,
Like russet torches in the forest depths.
I hear no splutter or crackle of resin,
Yet they burn and burn.

Does he see them,
Offering this last sacrifice of summer?
Does he see them in a different time,
Flower in fire,
And suddenly put on winter?

For us in exquisite slowness,
They turn in the cool embrace of Autumn.
In silent dance,
The leaves curl, blush, flame out,
In appalling submission,
To bring him this yearly gift of color,
amid the Autumn drab.

Lord, in my old age grant me
One last passionate flowering–
Let love burn off my summer green,
In sudden, splendid fire.

September Watercolor

Glenn Ward Dresbach

The willows drop the yellow leaves
They can no longer hold—
Irreverent, the blackbirds strut
Upon a cloth of gold.

Below them silver of a brook
Runs through a meadow strange
Too suddenly, and fades in blue,
Hazed atmosphere of change . . .

The airs are still, but here I feel
A movement in my heart
Like phantom hands reached out to stay
Beauty that must depart.

RED MOUNTAIN PASS
Between Silverton and Ouray, Colorado
Dick Dietrich Photography

Evening
of
Autumn

Luman Wesley Colton

When the dew falls on the cornfields
    And the mist lies in the vales
Like a wrinkled sheet at bedtime;
    And the calm of fall prevails
In the countryside so fruitful,
    Trees bend low with heavy load,
And the harvest moon comes looming
    Up beyond the tree-lined road;
When the maple leaves' first color
    Gives preview of what's to come,
And the rabbits meet to frolic
    In the land of rabbit-dom,
Then I catch my breath for wonder
    At the beauty of it all.
For I know, deep down inside me,
    That there is no time like fall.

HARVEST SUNRISE. Near Alpine, Oregon. Dennis Frates/Oregon Scenics.

Readers' Forum

Meet Our Ideals Readers and Their Families

Have you experienced a specific instance when God touched your life in a remarkable way? Perhaps a heartfelt prayer was answered or a burden miraculously lifted. The Ideals editors would like to hear your story. Send your typed description to: STORIES OF FAITH, C/O EDITORIAL DEPARTMENT, IDEALS MAGAZINE, P.O. BOX 305300, NASHVILLE, TENNESSEE 37230. *We're sorry, but the stories cannot be returned.*

MARY M. GALLAGHER of Port Orange, Florida, sent us this picture of her two great-grandchildren, Michelle Dillingham and Jon Michael Dillingham II. The two cousins met for the first time in April 1995. Traveling all the way from Würzberg, Germany, Michelle and her parents, Sergeant and Mrs. James Dillingham, joined Jon Michael and his parents, Jon and Diane Dillingham from Elyria, Ohio. Michelle, who was three years old at the time, and Jon Michael, then five years old, quickly became friends during their stay with their grandma, Betty Ward, in Port Orange.

Young Jessica, daughter of ED AND SHARON SHARROW, loves the colorful petunias, warm sunshine, and fresh smell of green grass in her front yard in Queensbury, New York. To help keep her out of trouble, her canine friend Kayoh is always by her side. On rainy days, Jessica enjoys looking at books and magazines, especially the pictures in *Ideals*.

THANK YOU Mary M. Gallagher and Ed and Sharon Sharrow for sharing with *Ideals*. We hope to hear from other readers who would like to share photos and stories with the *Ideals* family. Please include a self-addressed, stamped envelope if you would like the photos returned. Keep your original photographs for safekeeping and send duplicate photos along with your name, address, and telephone number to:

READERS' FORUM
IDEALS PUBLICATIONS INC.
P.O. BOX 305300
NASHVILLE, TENNESSEE
37230

ideals®

Publisher, Patricia A. Pingry
Editor, Lisa C. Ragan
Copy Editor, Michelle Prater Burke
Production Manager,
Tina Wells Davenport
Editorial Assistant, Tara E. Lynn
Editorial Intern, Melissa A. Chronister
Contributing Editors,
Lansing Christman, Deana Deck,
Pamela Kennedy, Patrick McRae,
Mary Skarmeas, Nancy Skarmeas

ACKNOWLEDGMENTS

MY DOG from *AROUND AND ABOUT* by Marchette Chute, copyright © 1957 by E. P. Dutton. SEPTEMBER WATERCOLOR by Glenn Ward Dresbach used by permission of the author's estate. THE FELLOWSHIP OF BOOKS from *WHEN DAY IS DONE* by Edgar A. Guest, copyright © 1921 by The Reilly & Lee Co. Used by permission of the author's estate. THE WALK TO SCHOOL from *LOVE AND LAUGHTER* by Marjorie Holmes. Copyright © 1967 by Marjorie Holmes Mighell. Used by permission of Doubleday, a division of Bantam Doubleday Dell Publishing Group, Inc. OLD THINGS from *THE GOLDEN ROAD* by Edna Jaques, copyright in Canada by Thomas Allen & Son Limited. INVITATION TO A GARDEN from *NEW ENGLAND HERITAGE AND OTHER POEMS* by Rose Koralewsky. Used by permission of Branden Publishing, Boston. DON'T GROW AWAY by Douglas Malloch used by permission of the author's estate. Our sincere thanks to the following authors whom we were unable to locate: Thomas Curtis Clark for THE TOUCH OF HUMAN HANDS, Tim Marks for OLD AGE, and Anna M. Priestley for UPON A ROCK.

Autumn Smiles

Beverly J. Anderson

Trees are standing proud and tall,
Dressed in finery for fall.
Maples wear their scarlet gowns;
Aspens don gold-glimmered crowns.

Meadows, hills, and gardens too
Sparkle with October's hue.

Lavish yellow, ripened days
Are rich with harvest-time displays.

Such delight in all we see
In glad Autumn's pageantry.
As her wonders we behold,
Autumn smiles in red and gold.